Instructor's Guide For

Nursing Leadership and Management: Concepts and Practices

Fourth Edition

D1466924

Instructor's Guide For

Nursing Leadership and Management: Concepts and Practices

Fourth Edition

Ruth M. Tappen, RN, EdD, FAAN
Professor
Florida Atlantic University
College of Nursing
Boca Raton, FL

 F. A. DAVIS Company • Philadelphia

F. A. Davis Company
1915 Arch Street
Philadelphia, PA 19103
www.fadavis.com

Last digit indicates print number: 10 9 8 7 6 5 4 3 2

Printed in the United States of America

ISBN 0–8036–0611–7

Contents

INTRODUCTION

SUGGESTIONS FOR USING THE
SPECIAL FEATURES OF THE FOURTH EDITION

The fourth edition has a number of features, several of which are new to this edition. The following are some suggestions for maximizing their use.

Outline. The outline serves to alert students to the information they will find in the chapter they are about to read. If they look it over before reading the chapter, they will have a better idea of what to expect and how the content is organized. The outline is also helpful in locating specific content in each of the chapters.

Learning Objectives. The objectives articulate what students can expect to have learned when they have completed the chapter.

Test Yourself. The primary purpose of this new feature is to stimulate interest in the content of the chapter and to get the reader to begin thinking about the subject of the chapter. It is not expected to be exhaustive and not meant to be a pretest that determines how much the reader knows about the subject before reading the chapter. The questions in the Instructor's Guide serve this latter purpose.

Quotations. The quotes that are set off from the rest of the text were selected to add depth to the content of the chapter. They provide additional commentary on the subject under discussion in the often colorful words used by well-known historical figures as well as contemporary authors.

Perspectives. Also a new feature, perspectives present different viewpoints, occasionally controversial viewpoints, on the subject under consideration to introduce readers to the often lively debates that occur in the field and to expose them to the variety of opinions that exist on many leadership and management subjects.

Case Studies. Another new feature of the fourth edition, the case studies provide an opportunity for students to apply leadership and management concepts to real-life situations, which is often difficult for students and particularly for those who have not yet been employed in a health care setting. Students may be asked to read and reflect on the case and write their responses to each of the questions before class. Their answers can be reviewed and discussed in class using the principles and concepts from both current and previous chapters. There is seldom a single correct way to handle the type of situation described in the case studies. Instead, they are designed to stimulate critical thinking and to help the student to apply concepts and principles to specific situations.

Research Examples. The research examples were chosen to reflect the wide variety of studies related to leadership and management, both qualitative and quantitative. Some are specific to nursing; others are classics: the famous Hawthorne studies; Lewin, Lippitt, and White's study of leadership styles; and one of the most interesting, "Being Sane in Insane Places." Sufficient information is provided to allow the reader to critique the design of the study and decide how much support it provides for the concepts and principles tested. As with other aspects of practice, there is a great need for more research related to nursing leadership and management.

USING THIS TEXT IN NURSING LEADERSHIP AND MANAGEMENT COURSES

Nursing leadership and management courses naturally differ across the United States and in other countries. Some emphasize leadership and others emphasize management. Placement within the curriculum varies as well. When the course is placed near the beginning of a program, there is often a return to the more complex topics near the end of the program.

To accommodate these variations, the book is divided into several units: an introductory unit, a unit focused on leadership, another focused on management, a fourth unit on more complex issues that span leadership and management, and, finally, a smaller unit on career development from a leadership and management perspective.

Several suggested outlines that can be used in various nursing curricula follow:

I.   Leadership-Focused Semester Course

Week 1	Chapter 1	Studying Leadership and Management
	Chapter 2	Conceptual Base for Leadership and Management
Week 2	Chapter 3	Components of Effective Leadership
	Chapter 4	Advanced Communication Styles: Conflict and Negotiation
Week 3	Chapter 5	Dynamics of Working Groups and Teams
	Chapter 6	Leading Workplace Meetings
Week 4	Chapter 7	Diversity in the Workplace
Week 5	Chapter 8	Time Management
	Chapter 9	Critically Reflective Thinking and Problem Solving
Week 6	Chapter 10	Leading Changes
Week 7	Chapter 12	Directing and Organizing Patient Care

Midterm

Week 8	Chapter 13	Individual Evaluation Procedures
Week 9	Chapter 18	Workplace Health and Safety
Week 10	Chapter 19	Quality Improvement
Week 11	Chapter 20	Workplace Ethics
Week 12	Chapter 21	Power, Empowerment, and Political Influence
Week 13	Chapter 22	Political and Economic Context of Health Care
Week 14	Chapter 23	Leadership Aspects of Career Development

Final Exam

I.   Management-Focused Semester Course

Week 1	Chapter 1	Studying Leadership and Management
	Chapter 2	Conceptual Base for Leadership and Management
Week 2	Chapter 3	Components of Effective Leadership
	Chapter 11	Components of Effective Management
Week 3	Chapter 4	Advanced Communication Styles: Conflict and Negotiation
	Chapter 7	Diversity in the Workplace
Week 4	Chapter 8	Time Management

III. Divided into: Basic (early in the curriculum) and Advanced (near the end of the curriculum)

The Basics of Leadership and Management

Advanced Leadership and Management

IV. Leadership and Management in an Integrated Curriculum

Introduction to Nursing

Fundamental Courses

Clinical Courses

Nursing Management or Senior Practicum

Senior Seminar

CHAPTER 1
STUDYING LEADERSHIP AND MANAGEMENT

I. CONTENT OUTLINE

WHY STUDY LEADERSHIP AND MANAGEMENT
Leadership and Management Defined
Leadership
Management
The Difference Between Management and Leadership

FOUNDATIONAL CONCEPTS FOR LEADERSHIP AND MANAGEMENT
Open Systems: The Interaction of People with Their Environment
System Defined
Hierarchy of Systems
Wholeness
Openness
Energy Fields
Growth
Patterns
Individuality
Sentience
Individual Factors Affecting Human Behavior
Assumptions about Human Behavior
Multiple Factors Influencing Behavior
Stress, Threatening Situations, and Behavior
Reflex Actions
Nondeliberative Mechanisms
Deliberative Mechanisms

SUMMARY

II. LEARNING OBJECTIVES

After completing this chapter, the reader will be able to:
- Discuss the value of studying leadership and management for the health care professional.
- Define and distinguish between leadership and management.
- Use an open systems framework when analyzing leadership and management situations.
- Recognize the use of nondeliberative and deliberative mechanisms to reduce stress and avoid threatening situations in the work environment.

III. NOTE TO INSTRUCTOR

This chapter introduces a number of basic leadership and management concepts. Some may be familiar to your students: open systems, human behavior, and stress. If so, they need to be reviewed only briefly in terms of their application to leadership and management. The first section, containing definitions of leadership and management and an explanation of the relationship between the two, should be reviewed carefully with students because there is much confusion in the literature and much misunderstanding about the differences between the two and how one is related to the other. The term "leader-manager" is introduced but has been dropped from regular use in the text because it may have contributed to this confusion, rather than helping students understand their interrelationship as had been intended.

IV. STUDENT LEARNING ACTIVITIES

A. Questions for Review and Discussion

1. Why is it important to understand the difference between leadership and management?
2. Describe a situation in which a person acted as a leader. Explain how you concluded that the person was a leader.
3. What do you believe most people think of when they use the word "leader" to describe someone?
4. Why should leaders and managers be concerned about the way people react to stress?
5. Review the list of deliberative mechanisms and divide them into two categories: "healthy" and "unhealthy." What rationale did you use to categorize them?
6. What is the difference between a mechanistic and an organic view of the world? How does this difference in viewpoint affect the way people lead and manage others?
7. Create a hierarchy of systems beginning with the individual students in your class and expanding to the entire nation and the world.
8. Identify several patterns of behavior that have developed in your classroom. How are they helpful or unhelpful to members of the class and to the instructor?

B. Projects/Assignments

1. Write a half-page description of a nurse manager who thinks holistically and a second half-page description of a nurse manager who thinks mechanistically (reductionistically). On the second page of this assignment, compare and contrast the two approaches and discuss which framework you prefer and why.
2. Describe a highly stressful situation in which you were involved or one that you observed firsthand. List all the people who were present (use initials or titles, not names) and describe how each behaved during and after the event. Who, in your opinion, responded effectively during the crisis? Who, in your opinion, was least effective? What leadership-related lesson can you draw from this?

CHAPTER 2
CONCEPTUAL BASE FOR
LEADERSHIP AND MANAGEMENT

I. CONTENT OUTLINE

THEORY
Why have a theory?
Organization
Perspective
Explanation
Prediction
Application
Theory Selection

EARLY LEADERSHIP THEORIES
Trait Theories
Great Man Theory
Individual Characteristics
Trait Studies
Comment
Behavioral Theories
Authoritarian, Democratic, and Laissez-Faire Styles (Lewin, Lippitt, and White)
Leader Behavior Descriptions (Hemphill; Halpin, and Winer)
Task versus Relationship Orientation (Blake and Mouton)

EARLY MANAGEMENT THEORIES
Scientific Management
Human Relations

CONTEMPORARY THEORIES
Motivational Theories
Hierarchy of Needs (Maslow)
Theory X and Y (Mc Gregor)
Hygiene and Motivation Factors (Herzberg)
Theory Z (Ouchi)
Behavioral Management (Miller)
Comment
Situational Theories
Contingency Theory (Fiedler)
Path-Goal Theory (House)
Situational Determinants
Interactional Theories
Elements of a Leader Situation (Hollander)
Leader-Group Interaction (Schreisheim, Mowby, and Stogdill)

Complex Man and Organizations (Schein)
Transformational Leadership
Transformational Factors
Transactional Factors
Nonleadership Factors
SUMMARY

II. LEARNING OBJECTIVES

After completing this chapter, the reader will be able to:
- Trace the evolution of early leadership and management theories.
- Distinguish a simplistic leadership or management theory from a comprehensive theory.
- Evaluate the degree to which the major theories include the basic elements of leadership and management situations.
- Compare and contrast the Democratic style to the Authoritarian and Laissez-Faire styles, Theory X to Theories Y and Z, Task Orientation to Relationship Orientation, and the humanistic approach to the Behavioral Management approach.
- Discuss the effect of one's choice of theories on the practice of leadership and management.

III. NOTE TO INSTRUCTOR

This is a long, complex chapter. Most students will need some help sorting out the various theories and facing the increasing complexity of these theories. Figure 2–1 should be referred to frequently as a guide to the many theories discussed. The chapter begins with the simplest explanations of leadership and management and proceeds to the most complex at the end. You can also encourage students to read critically: Does this theory support what I've observed? Is it useful to me in practice? Is it supported by research?

The goal is to expose students to the richness of leadership and management thought and to develop an understanding of the basis for most recommendations for increasing one's effectiveness as a leader and/or manager. Some students may be uncomfortable with the fact that there is no single answer to the question of what makes a person an effective leader or manager. Others may be challenged to explore these questions further.

Taking the stance of the critical thinker can lead to some lively discussions and debates about these theories. The suggested student activities reflect these possibilities.

IV. STUDENT LEARNING ACTIVITIES

A. Questions for Review and Discussion:

1. Why do scholars develop theories?
2. Of what use is a leadership or management theory to the practicing nurse, leader, or manager?
3. What makes a particular theory helpful to you? What should you look for in a theory?
4. Why are the early leadership theories described as limited? What is missing in them?
5. How have leadership and management theories addressed the issue of women in management? How do you think this issue should be addressed?
6. What similarities can you find in the Authoritarian-Democratic-Laissez-Faire, Leader Behavior and Task versus Relationship Theories? How are they different?
7. Have you encountered Maslow's Hierarchy of Needs in other courses? How does Maslow's Hierarchy relate to leadership and management? What is the difference between applications to patient care and applications to leadership and management?
8. Compare Theories X, Y, and Z to the leadership style theories. How are they similar? How do they differ?
9. Compare Miller's Behavioral Management to Taylor's Scientific Management. In what ways are they similar? To what extent are Taylor's principles still influential today?
10. In what way(s) are the Situational Theories more complex than the earlier ones?
11. What is an LPC? How does this idea relate to management effectiveness?
12. What do people usually mean when they talk about the "Hawthorne Effect"? What did the Hawthorne studies actually show?
13. What distinguishes the interactional theories from the others? Critique them in terms of the open systems theory principles from Chapter 1. How are they less mechanistic than earlier theories?
14. Why do you think the Transformational Theory is popular in nursing? Why is having and sharing a vision important?
15. What would you add to these existing theories? Would you make them simpler or more complex? Why?

B. Projects/Assignments

1. Role-play a staff meeting in which you are the first-line manager who must resolve a productivity problem. Paperwork is not being done on time by your staff and your supervisor is pressuring you to make sure that all charting is 100 percent complete and accurate. Try using Ouchi's Theory Z approach in the first role play, then Miller's Behavioral Management and Bass and Avolio's Transformational Leadership in a second and third role play. Evaluate the effect of the three selected approaches on the outcome.
2. Read the original account (available in most libraries) by Lewin, Lippitt and White of the research that provided the bases for the Authoritarian, Democratic, and Laissez-Faire styles of leadership. Critique their account of the research. (You can do this with the Research Example instead, but the original account is preferable.)

3. Role-play three different leadership styles. Select three students who are willing to lead groups and have them select the Authoritarian, Democratic, or Laissez-Faire style by drawing slips of paper from a hat. On each slip of paper, list one of the styles and the group's goal: to create a collage representing the nursing profession. Divide the remainder of the class into three groups to be led by the three volunteers (double or triple the number of groups for larger classes). Provide each group with paper, scissors, and paste but no instructions. Allow the groups 20 minutes to work together. Then, ask the class to vote for the "best" product and ask each group to comment on the leadership and how the group functioned. What did you learn about leadership styles?

4. Debate whether leaders are "born" or "made." Select six students, three for the pro side and three for the con side. Allow each person two minutes to present his or her argument and one minute for rebuttal. Ask the remainder of the class, who observed the debate, to vote for the most persuasive team. Then, discuss the issue with the class: Are leaders born or made?

5. List as many elements as possible that you think should be included in a leadership or management theory (choose one or the other). Then create a diagram such as Figure 1–1 or 2–2 to graphically illustrate the interrelationship of these elements.

CHAPTER 3
COMPONENTS OF EFFECTIVE LEADERSHIP

I. CONTENT OUTLINE

KNOWLEDGE
Leadership Knowledge
Nursing Knowledge
Critical Thinking

SELF-AWARENESS
Importance of Self-Awareness
Increasing Self-Awareness

COMMUNICATION
Active Listening
Encouraging a Flow of Information
Assertiveness
Seeking and Providing Feedback
Linking
Networking

ENERGY
Neural and Emotional Energy
Energy and Leadership Effectiveness
Energy Flow and Reserves
Energy Inventory

GOALS
Goal Levels
Meaningful Goals
Communicating a Vision
Clarity and Congruence

ACTION
Working with Others
Initiating Action
Decision-Making Professional Activities

LEADERSHIP EFFECTIVENESS CHECKLIST

SUMMARY

II. LEARNING OBJECTIVES

After completing this chapter, the reader will be able to:
- Name the components of effective leadership.
- Discuss the importance of each component of effective leadership.
- Evaluate personal leadership effectiveness in terms of the components of effective leadership.
- Evaluate other leaders in terms of the components of effective leadership.

III. NOTE TO INSTRUCTOR

For most students, this will be a relatively easy chapter to read and understand. The six components are different aspects of a unitary phenomenon: effective leadership. Any one component alone will not produce effective leadership, but in concert they will. The more sophisticated reader will recognize the open-systems, humanistic foundation on which they are based, but most students will need to have this pointed out to them.

The focus of this chapter is the student: the degree to which he or she is an effective leader and what each one can do to increase his or her effectiveness now and in the future. The checklist is key to achieving this goal. It is meant to be a guide to thoughtful self-evaluation and to help students identify the areas in which improvement is needed.

IV. STUDENT LEARNING ACTIVITIES

A. Questions for Review and Discussion

1. What are the six components of effective leadership?
2. What types of knowledge are needed to be an effective nurse leader? Why is each one important?
3. How does self-awareness affect a person's effectiveness as a leader? How can you increase your own self-awareness?
4. Why was communication described as being "at the heart of leadership"? Review some of the principles for effective communication that you learned in other courses and discuss how they can be applied to leadership situations.
5. What types of communication distinguish a leader from a non-leader?
6. Why is networking considered so important in leadership? How can you use it to increase your effectiveness? How does a person "network"? What can you do to enlarge your network?
7. Are goals more important in a work environment than in social settings? Why or why not?
8. What is the best way for a leader to set goals for a group? Why?
9. What type of "visions" could a nurse leader share with a patient-care team?

B. Projects/Assignments

1. Complete the Leadership Effectiveness Checklist for yourself. Write a two-page paper evaluating your present effectiveness and outlining a plan for improving your effectiveness.

2. At the end of a day spent in a clinical setting, evaluate your leadership effectiveness using the checklist at the end of Chapter 3. Identify three areas of particular strength and three in which you need to improve. Develop a personal plan for improvement in the weakness areas and four ways to capitalize on your strengths.

3. Using the Leadership Effectiveness Checklist, observe a nurse manager, supervisor, or other management-level individual in a clinical setting. Evaluate this person's effectiveness as a leader, considering ways in which the environment, type of work, and characteristics of the staff impact on this person's effectiveness.

4. Using Table 3–1 as a guide, write a scenario in which group, organization, and leader goals differ. Describe the situation in a concise example and create a diagram in the same manner as Table 3–1 to illustrate the differences in goals at different system levels.

5. Complete a personal energy inventory for 7 days using the forms that follow; then answer the questions on page 64. Do you find yourself with an energy deficit at the end of most days? What energy drains could you eliminate? What energy boosters could you add or increase? What other patterns do you see in your personal inventory? (If you work nights, you may want to change the times on the tables and graphs before doing this.)

Monday

Primary Activity	Energy Rating
7 A.M.	
9 A.M.	
11 A.M.	
1 P.M.	
3 P.M.	
4 P.M.	
5 P.M.	
7 P.M.	
9 P.M.	
11 P.M.	

Tuesday

Primary Activity	Energy Rating
7 A.M.	
9 A.M.	
11 A.M.	
1 P.M.	
3 P.M.	
4 P.M.	
5 P.M.	
7 P.M.	
9 P.M.	
11 P.M.	

Wednesday

Primary Activity	Energy Rating
7 A.M.	
9 A.M.	
11 A.M.	
1 P.M.	
3 P.M.	
4 P.M.	
5 P.M.	
7 P.M.	
9 P.M.	
11 P.M.	

Thursday

Primary Activity	Energy Rating
7 A.M.	
9 A.M.	
11 A.M.	
1 P.M.	
3 P.M.	
4 P.M.	
5 P.M.	
7 P.M.	
9 P.M.	
11 P.M.	

Friday

Primary Activity	Energy Rating
7 A.M.	
9 A.M.	
11 A.M.	
1 P.M.	
3 P.M.	
4 P.M.	
5 P.M.	
7 P.M.	
9 P.M.	
11 P.M.	

Saturday

Primary Activity	Energy Rating
7 A.M.	
9 A.M.	
11 A.M.	
1 P.M.	
3 P.M.	
4 P.M.	
5 P.M.	
7 P.M.	
9 P.M.	
11 P.M.	

Sunday

Primary Activity	Energy Rating
7 A.M.	
9 A.M.	
11 A.M.	
1 P.M.	
3 P.M.	
4 P.M.	
5 P.M.	
7 P.M.	
9 P.M.	
11 P.M.	

Personal Energy Inventory

Monday

	7 A.M.	9 A.M.	11 A.M.	1 P.M.	3 P.M.	5 P.M.	7 P.M.	9 P.M.	11 P.M.
+5									
4									
2									
1									
0									
1									
2									
3									
4									
-5									

Tuesday

	7 A.M.	9 A.M.	11 A.M.	1 P.M.	3 P.M.	5 P.M.	7 P.M.	9 P.M.	11 P.M.
+5									
4									
2									
1									
0									
1									
2									
3									
4									
-5									

Wednesday

	7 A.M.	9 A.M.	11 A.M.	1 P.M.	3 P.M.	5 P.M.	7 P.M.	9 P.M.	11 P.M.
+5									
4									
2									
1									
0									
1									
2									
3									
4									
-5									

Thursday

	7 A.M.	9 A.M.	11 A.M.	1 P.M.	3 P.M.	5 P.M.	7 P.M.	9 P.M.	11 P.M.
+5									
4									
2									
1									
0									
1									
2									
3									
4									
-5									

Friday

	7 A.M.	9 A.M.	11 A.M.	1 P.M.	3 P.M.	5 P.M.	7 P.M.	9 P.M.	11 P.M.
+5									
4									
2									
1									
0									
1									
2									
3									
4									
-5									

Saturday

	7 A.M.	9 A.M.	11 A.M.	1 P.M.	3 P.M.	5 P.M.	7 P.M.	9 P.M.	11 P.M.
+5									
4									
2									
1									
0									
1									
2									
3									
4									
-5									

Sunday

	7 A.M.	9 A.M.	11 A.M.	1 P.M.	3 P.M.	5 P.M.	7 P.M.	9 P.M.	11 P.M.
+5									
4									
2									
1									
0									
1									
2									
3									
4									
-5									

CHAPTER 4
ADVANCED COMMUNICATION SKILLS: CONFLICT AND NEGOTIATION

I. CONTENT OUTLINE

SOURCES OF CONFLICT

PREVENTIVE MEASURES

CONFRONTATION
Avoidance of Confrontation
Confronting Another Person
Cautions

RESPONDING TO CONFLICT

NEGOTIATION
Setting the Stage
Key Issues

INFORMAL NEGOTIATIONS
Opening Move
Continuing the Negotiation
Reaching Agreement

FORMAL NEGOTIATION
Opening Move
Continuing the Negotiation
Reaching Agreement
Strategies to Influence the Process

SUMMARY

II. LEARNING OBJECTIVES

- After completing this chapter, the reader will be able to:
- List common sources of conflict in a work situation.
- Discuss strategies for creating a climate in which conflicts can be more readily resolved.
- Identify situations in which negotiation would be useful.

- Use confrontation techniques appropriately.
- Apply the informal negotiation process to everyday work situations.
- Participate in formal negotiations in the workplace.

III. NOTE TO INSTRUCTOR

Instructors who have used previous editions of this textbook will note that the discussion of the basic communication techniques has been condensed because it is repeated so often in many other nursing courses and textbooks. Instead, advanced communication techniques, which are essential to leadership, are presented in detail. Most readers will have encountered some content in assertiveness and confrontation before, but it is unlikely that they are familiar with the information about negotiation.

As with most leadership and management content, reading about it is just the beginning of learning. Practice in applying these concepts and principles is essential and can be done both in the classroom and in clinical settings. Some suggestions for doing this follow, but you will find many additional opportunities to apply these principles as you work with your students in the classroom and in clinical settings.

IV. STUDENT LEARNING ACTIVITIES

A. Questions for Review and Discussion:

1. What are the most common sources of conflict on a health care team? Why do these conflicts occur?
2. What can a nurse leader do to prevent conflicts from (a) occurring (b) escalating? What preventive measures would be unadvisable?
3. Why do some people avoid confrontation? What usually happens when they do this?
4. What is the difference between "I" messages and "You" messages? Give some examples of each and analyze the difference in terms of what is communicated and what type of response can be expected.
5. Explain the difference between accommodation and consolidation. Which is preferable? Why?
6. Describe the informal negotiation process. When would you use this process instead of the formal process? Give a few examples.
7. Why is the opening move considered so critical in a formal negotiation? What is the most effective opening move? Why?
8. How is agreement reached in a formal negotiation? What type of agreement is the goal?
9. What strategies are especially helpful in conducting a negotiation? Which ones should be avoided or used with great caution?
10. Why is it sometimes better to leave threats unspoken?

B. Projects/Assignments

1. Role-play a confrontation between a nurse manager and a licensed practical nurse who is habitually late but is also a very caring, technically skilled team member. If possible, videotape (alternatively, audiotape) the meeting role-play so that the class and the role players can critique the confrontation. Be sure that the group does not become too critical of the role players, but encourage honest reactions by reviewing principles for providing effective feedback (see Chapter 13) before proceeding with analysis of the tape.

2. Describe a confrontation you observed in the clinical setting. Include the people involved, who confronted whom and how it was done, and the response from the person confronted. Referring to the suggestions and cautions in Chapter 4, evaluate the strategies used by the confronter. Discuss the outcome of the confrontation and how it could have been done more effectively, if appropriate.

3. With a colleague or classmate, role-play a negotiation session with your immediate supervisor in which you are requesting a substantial salary increase based on merit.

CHAPTER 5
DYNAMICS OF WORKING GROUPS AND TEAMS

I. CONTENT OUTLINE

SMALL GROUPS
Common Bonds
Groups as Open Systems

STAGES OF GROUP DEVELOPMENT
Forming
Individual Tasks
Group Tasks
Climate and Behavior
Leadership
Storming
Individual Tasks
Group Tasks
Climate and Behavior
Leadership
Norming
Individual Tasks
Group Tasks
Climate and Behavior
Leadership
Performing
Individual Tasks
Group Tasks
Climate and Behavior
Leadership
Adjourning
Individual Tasks
Group Tasks
Climate and Behavior
Leadership
Different Perspectives on Group Stages

DIMENSIONS OF GROUP PROCESS

HIDDEN AGENDAS
Sources
Leader Response

DYSFUNCTIONAL GROUP INTERACTIONS
Social Loafing
Groupthink
Polarization
Scapegoating

TEAM BUILDING
Select Team Members
Set Goals
Define Roles
Develop Identity and Cohesiveness
Definition
Territory
Connections
Esprit de Corps
Guide Decision Making
Default
Authority
Minority
Majority Vote
Consensus
Unanimous Consent
Selection of a Decision-Making Mode
Influence Group Norms
Encourage Frequent and Open Communication
Manage Conflicts
Communication with Other Teams

ADVANTAGES OF TEAMWORK

DISADVANTAGES OF TEAMWORK

SUMMARY

II. LEARNING OBJECTIVES
After completing this chapter, the reader will be able to:
- Define the term *group* and describe characteristics of groups as open systems.
- List the five stages of group development and describe the group climate, individual and group tasks, and appropriate leader actions for each stage.
- Identify hidden agendas and dysfunctional interactions in small groups.
- Use the seven dimensions of group process to analyze a work group's dynamics.
- Build an effective nursing or interdisciplinary health care team.
- Discuss the advantages and disadvantages of teamwork.

III. NOTE TO INSTRUCTOR
The dynamics of a small group can be amazingly complex. Some of what happens in a small group is obvious to everyone, but so much is either subtle or hidden altogether that only a knowledgeable observer can detect it. There is considerable detail in this chapter about what to look for and how to respond to what is observed. However, nothing can substitute for real-life group experience in which

the student can see, hear, and feel the dynamics of the group. There are many ways in which you can provide this real-life experience: classroom role playing, group projects that include analysis of the dynamics of the process of completing the project, clinical group seminars, and so forth.

Teams are a special form of group. Most health care professionals work as part of one or more teams, yet many are poorly prepared for teamwork. Often a nurse is in a position to help other team members work more effectively together. This chapter is full of practical suggestions for improving groups and teams.

IV. STUDENT LEARNING ACTIVITIES

A. Questions for Review and Discussion

1. How does a small number of people become a group?
2. What has to happen to individuals to make each one a member of this group?
3. Why is it important to think of a group as an open system?
4. What characteristics of open systems (from Chapter 1) are especially important to keep in mind when leading or joining a group?
5. Name the five stages of group development. For each of these five stages of group development, describe the usual tasks faced by the group and the typical group climate. Then identify the actions taken by the leader to facilitate group development.
6. What are some of the objections to the five stages of group development described in this chapter? Use open-systems concepts in your critique of these objections.
7. Compare the seven dimensions of group process with the five stages of group development: Are they congruent? Is there any conflict between these two frameworks for understanding group dynamics?
8. What is a hidden agenda? How can you identify them? Why do they occur? How should a leader deal with them?
9. Why does group interaction become dysfunctional at times?
10. Which of the four dysfunctional patterns described in this chapter do you think is the most harmful? Why?
11. If you were asked to form a new patient-care team, what criteria would you use to choose team members? How would you build team identity and cohesion?
12. Define each of the six ways a group can use to reach a decision. Which of these six is preferable in most cases? Why?
13. Discuss the advantages and disadvantages of teamwork. Do the advantages outweigh the disadvantages? When and why is it preferable to work in a team rather than independently? When is working independently preferable?

B. Projects/Assignments

1. Write a scenario similar to the school meningitis outbreak example, illustrating how a group forms, storms, develops norms, performs, and finally adjourns.
2. Attend a committee meeting, either at school or at work. Identify the stages of group development, the task(s) the group is working on, leader behaviors, hidden agendas, and any dysfunctional interaction patterns that appear.

3. Analyze your clinical group in terms of both the stages of group development and the characteristics of a team. To what extent has your group become a team?
4. Ask several colleagues or health care professionals in your clinical setting how much of their time is spent working as part of a team and how much time is spent working independently. Then ask them which they prefer and why. Collate the results and compare with the advantages and disadvantages of teamwork presented in Chapter 5.

CHAPTER 6
LEADING WORKPLACE MEETINGS

I. CONTENT OUTLINE

PURPOSE OF WORKPLACE MEETINGS
Informational Meetings
Problem-Solving Meetings
Issue-Focused Meetings

GROUP ROLES
Functional Task Roles
Functional Group-Building Roles
Nonfunctional Roles

COMMUNICATION PATTERNS
One-Way
Stilted
Limited
Open
Chaotic

LEADING MEETINGS
Pre-Meeting Preparation
Agenda
Time
Place
Participants
Additional Factors to Consider
Implementation
Opening the Meeting
Guiding the Discussion
Concluding a Meeting
Follow-Up

ATTENDING MEETINGS
Pre-Meeting Preparation
Implementation
Opening the Meeting
Participating in the Discussion
Concluding a Meeting
Follow-Up

SCRIPT

SCRIPT ANALYSIS
Sociogram
Seating Arrangement

Communication Pattern
Roles Played by Group Members
Maturity of the Group
Course of the Discussion, Decision Making, and Outcome
Leadership Style and Effectiveness
SUMMARY

II. LEARNING OBJECTIVES

After completing this chapter, the reader will be able to:
- Discuss the various purposes of workplace meetings.
- Distinguish between functional and nonfunctional group roles at meetings.
- Identify communication patterns within small groups.
- Lead informational, problem-solving, and issue-focused meetings.
- Participate in meetings in a constructive manner.

III. NOTE TO INSTRUCTOR

In many ways, this chapter is an extension of the content in Chapter 5. More detail on group dynamics is offered, particularly information on specific behaviors of leaders and group participants. There is also some practical information about meetings, with an emphasis on making the time spent in meetings as worthwhile as possible.

Everyone has had some experience with meetings, so most students should find this content relatively easy to relate to and to understand. Having a framework for understanding what is happening in a meeting is valuable to group members as well as to the designated leader. It is important to point out that leadership is a shared responsibility and does not belong to the leader alone. As the case study demonstrates, the script that is included in this chapter can be used for many purposes and analyzed from different perspectives. Even more interesting would be to create a script from a meeting your students attended and analyze it as demonstrated in this chapter.

IV. STUDENT LEARNING ACTIVITIES

A. Questions for Review and Discussion

1. Do you think people enjoy going to meetings? Why or why not?
2. What are the three primary purposes for holding a meeting in a health care setting? Give an example of each type of meeting.
3. What is the difference between functional and nonfunctional roles played by people in meetings? Between task and group building roles? Relate this to the behavioral leadership theories (Chapter 2).
4. Give three examples of functional task roles, functional group building roles and nonfunctional roles. What might a person playing each of these roles say during a meeting?
5. Why are both the one-way and chaotic patterns of communication of limited effectiveness?
6. What pattern of communication is generally the most desirable? Why?

7. When planning a meeting, what do you need to do ahead of time? What should you do if you will be attending the meeting?
8. What should the leader do during a meeting? What should the leader avoid doing?
9. What are some typical leadership problems that arise during a meeting? How should the leader handle them?
10. What is the responsibility of a participant in a meeting?
11. What is meant by follow-up after a meeting? Why is it important? What are the potential consequences of failing to follow up?

B. Projects/Assignments

1. Attend a public meeting in your community or a committee meeting at school. Draw a sociogram of the meeting and analyze the meeting as illustrated in Chapter 6. Write a commentary to share with the class.
2. Conduct a mock problem-solving conference using either a patient/client problem or a typical nursing team problem as the focus. A volunteer leader and five or six team members is a good size for the group. Assign functional roles to half of the team and nonfunctional roles to the other half (not known to the leader) to play in the session. Analyze the outcomes as was done for the script, including a sociogram, seating arrangement, communication pattern, roles played, maturity of the group, course of discussion, decision making and the outcome, dominant synchronizers, and leadership style and effectiveness.
3. Plan a 10-minute information conference. Work through all phases of the design from a statement of purpose through evaluation. Assess both your effectiveness and the degree to which following the phases in development did or did not help you plan and implement an effective information conference.
4. Alternatively, role-play an issue-focused meeting called to discuss a policy change: Day-shift nurses will be asked to rotate to evenings or nights one week of every four beginning next week. Critique as described above.
5. If the equipment is available, videotape the mock conferences or meetings so that the class can review what happened and fast-forward or reverse to critical moments during the meetings. Critique as described above.
6. Select or create five complex but abstract designs from art reproductions or magazine advertisements. Divide the class into groups of five to seven people and ask them to select a leader. Give each leader a design to *verbally* describe to the group (group members are not shown the designs). Each group member is asked to freehand-draw the design as verbally directed by the leader. Give members 15 minutes to complete the designs, then ask them to display the designs on the board or tape them on the wall. Discuss the experience with the class (you can ask the class to rate the best, i.e., most accurate drawings).

CHAPTER 7
DIVERSITY IN THE WORKPLACE

I. CONTENT OUTLINE

DIVERSITY IN NURSING
In the Past
Today

NEED FOR SENSITIVITY
Is There a Problem?
Culture and Nursing

UNDERSTANDING DIFFERENCES IN SHARED MEANING
Kluckhohn's Model
Additional Important Differences

WORKING WITH PEOPLE OF DIVERSE CULTURES

LEADING AND MANAGING A DIVERSE WORKFORCE
Basic Do's and Don'ts
Cultural Awareness
Increasing Contact Between Groups
Informal Support Systems and Networks
Requiring Fairness and Prohibiting Discrimination

SUMMARY

II. LEARNING OBJECTIVES

After completing this chapter the reader will be able to:
- Describe trends in diversity in the nursing workforce.
- Discuss the importance of sensitivity to differences across diverse groups in the workplace.
- Identify cultural influence on beliefs, values, and behavior.
- Critique approaches to increasing sensitivity.
- Suggest strategies to improve working relationships among people from diverse groups.

III. NOTE TO INSTRUCTOR

Diversity is a subject that needs to be addressed with a great deal of sensitivity to the different experiences and feelings of the various students in the class. This is not as simple as it appears because (1) it is so easy to fall into the trap of stereotyping and generalizations, and (2) many people are unaware of the assumptions they have about people of differing ages, genders, ethnic groups, disabilities, and so forth. There are many opportunities for the teacher of nursing leadership and management to act as an exemplary role model. With this content, it is especially important to demonstrate your respect for others' cultural beliefs and values so that your students will follow suit.

IV. STUDENT LEARNING ACTIVITIES

A. Questions for Review and Discussion

1. What is the trend (increase or decrease) in terms of diversity in the nursing profession? Is it the same as the general population?
2. Which two groups were the primary targets of discriminatory practices in the nursing profession in the past?
3. Define culture. What is cultural sensitivity?
4. How would you go about identifying a need for increased cultural understanding and sensitivity in a health care setting?
5. What are the five dimensions of Kluckhohn's Model of Shared Meaning? Give an example of the variations possible in each dimension.
6. What are some other differences in beliefs, values, and behavior across cultures that are of particular interest to leaders and managers?
7. Review the five do's and don'ts for managing diversity in the workplace. Give examples of each do and don't.
8. Describe a generic program for increasing cultural sensitivity in the workplace.
9. How does the law support fairness and equal opportunity for all employees?

B. Projects/Assignments

1. Interview a nurse or other health care worker from a culture different from your own. Make up a list of open-ended questions after rereading the section on cultural differences in Chapter 7. You might want to ask about the person's reasons for working, types of satisfaction gained from working, aspirations, status of nurses in other countries, and so forth. Compare the answers with your own cultural perspective and with information about your respective culture found in the literature.
2. Interview several classmates or friends of a different culture than your own. Ask them to describe their idea of an "ideal employee." Identify the differences and similarities in their answers. To what extent did their cultural background seem to affect their answers? To what extent did their professional identification (e.g., nursing) and individual preferences and experiences influence their answers?
3. Compare the culture of a helping profession like nursing to the culture of a business-oriented profession such as accounting. What differences in beliefs, values and behaviors would you expect to find when comparing members of these two professions? What similarities would you expect to find?
4. Design a creative cultural sensitivity program for a nursing care unit. To what extent would the fact that these people work closely together every day affect your plan? What evidence would you look for that the program was effective? Share your plan with the class.

5. Role-play a scenario in which a nursing-care team consisting of one nurse and one patient-care assistant who speak different languages is attempting to teach a patient how to handle his new colostomy.

CHAPTER 8
TIME MANAGEMENT

I. CONTENT OUTLINE

THE TYRANNY OF TIME
Differing Time Perceptions
Hurry Sickness

HOW NURSES SPEND THEIR TIME
Lists
Tickler Files
Schedules and Blocks of Time
Time Lines
Filing Systems

SETTING LIMITS
Saying "No"
Eliminating Unnecessary Work
Keeping Goals Reasonable
Delegating

STREAMLINING WORK ACTIVITIES
Keeping A Time Log
Reducing Interruptions
Dealing with Recurrent Crises
Categorizing Activities
Finding the Fastest Way
Automating Repetitive Tasks

ENHANCING PRODUCTIVITY THROUGH LEADERSHIP

SUMMARY

II. LEARNING OBJECTIVES

After completing this chapter, the reader will be able to:
- Characterize his or her perception of time.
- Set short- and long term personal and career goals.
- Analyze activities at work using a time log.
- Organize and streamline work to make more effective use of available time.
- Set limits on the demands made on his or her time.

III. NOTE TO INSTRUCTOR

Most of us have time-management concerns. Unfortunately, it is far easier to talk about better management of our time than to actively make changes in the way we allocate our time both at work and outside of work hours. There are several ways to help students move to this application stage of learning: (1) identify time-wasting routines and behaviors in their clinical setting, (2) encourage students to complete their time logs and seriously analyze how they could use their time more effectively, (3) ask students to design more creative ways to make patient care routines not only more efficient but also more effective. You can also share your own timesavers and ask students to share theirs. These will be even more meaningful because they are also personalized.

IV. STUDENT LEARNING ACTIVITIES

A. Questions for Review and Discussion

1. What is your concept of time? Is it circular or linear? (Refer to "Test Yourself" at the beginning of this chapter.)
2. Do you think your time perspective differs from that of your classmates or colleagues in the clinical setting? In what way?
3. What is "hurry sickness"? Why is it potentially harmful? To what extent do you suffer from it? What can you do to counteract it?
4. How can something as simple as a list help you manage your time?
5. What is a tickler file? How could it help you manage your time?
6. Why is it sometimes necessary to set aside a block of time to complete a task? What makes this difficult to accomplish?
7. How much of your time is scheduled (i.e., your class schedule)? How does this affect the rest of your time allocation?
8. How do schedules help? Interfere?
9. How often do you say no when asked to do something? Is this too often or not often enough? When is it easy to do this? When is it difficult?
10. When goals are unreasonable, what can you do about it?
11. In what ways is delegation a time management strategy?
12. What are some ways a staff nurse can reduce the problem of interruptions? Give examples.
13. What are "recurrent crises"? How can a nurse manager reduce them? Improve unit response to them? Examples?
14. How does clustering or categorizing of activities help a nurse manage his or her time? Can you give an example?
15. When is automation helpful in time management?
16. What precautions are necessary when automating a task? Have you seen any examples of effective automation of repetitive tasks? Have you seen any examples of ineffective use of automation?
17. How can effective leadership improve time management?

B. Projects/Assignments

1. Complete the Test Yourself questions at the beginning of Chapter 8 with a classmate. Is your concept of time circular or linear? Did the list accurately reflect the way you perceive time?

2. Complete the time log in Chapter 8 for a full week. What types of patterns emerge? Are you satisfied with the way you manage your time? What would you change?

3. How do experienced nurses manage their time? Ask two or three nurses who seem to accomplish a great deal without appearing harried how they manage their time. Ask them to describe a typical day. Find out how they handle interruptions and crises and whether or not they feel they have enough time to accomplish all they want in a day.

4. Write two imaginative scenarios describing:
   a. a nurse manager with a serious case of "hurry sickness" and
   b. a nurse manager who has been "cured" of hurry sickness

5. List three specific changes you could make to improve the way you manage your time. Describe the barriers to making these changes. How can you overcome these barriers?

CHAPTER 9
CRITICALLY REFLECTIVE THINKING
AND PROBLEM SOLVING

I. CONTENT OUTLINE

CRITICALLY REFLECTIVE THINKING
Barriers to Clear Thinking
Assumptions
Mindsets
Circular Reasoning
Overgeneralizations and Stereotypes
Jumping to Conclusions
Misuse of Statistics
Mistaking Relationship for Cause and Effect
Allowing Emotion to Rule
Defining Critically Reflective Thinking
Examples of Muddy Thinking from Health Care
An Example from Leadership
Critical Analysis: A Guide
The Risk in Being a Critical Thinker

PROBLEM SOLVING
Steps in the Process
Enhancing Problem Solving
Ineffective Habits
Individual Differences

SUMMARY

II. LEARNING OBJECTIVES

After completing this chapter, the reader will be able to:
- Distinguish between clear and muddy thinking.
- Discuss common barriers to clear thinking.
- Define critically reflective thinking.
- Use critically reflective thinking in analyzing questions related to nursing leadership and management.
- Define problem solving and compare it with the nursing process.
- Use problem solving to resolve difficult leadership and management situations.

III. NOTE TO INSTRUCTOR

In this chapter, students are challenged to think about thinking. Muddy thinking is rampant, not only in health care but across our society. Yet we desperately need clear thinkers, particularly those who can also clearly articulate their concerns and positions.

Once introduced to the ideas contained in this chapter, students can actively participate in identifying instances of muddy thinking: in the media, in health care, in leadership and management situations. It is also helpful to encourage them to analyze why this muddy thinking has occurred. Is it sheer laziness? An ulterior motive? Need for a paradigm shift? Application of the principles of critically reflective thinking and problem solving can be both challenging and exciting for inquisitive students if we show them how valuable these skills are.

IV. STUDENT LEARNING ACTIVITIES

A. Questions for Review and Discussion

1. How do assumptions and mindsets affect our thinking and decision-making processes? Why is it so difficult to recognize this effect?
2. Explain circular reasoning. How does it contribute to muddy thinking? Likewise, explain and give examples of the effects of:
   a. overgeneralizations
   b. jumping to conclusions
   c. misuse of statistics
   d. mistaking a relationship for cause and effect
   e. allowing emotions to rule in our thinking and decision making.
3. Define critically reflective thinking.
4. What is a paradigm? How does it affect our decision making? Give at least two examples from health care and two from leadership.
5. List the five steps of critical analysis and give an example of how they can be used in a leadership or management situation.
6. What kind of risks does a critical thinker face? Are they worth it? How can they be reduced?
7. Define problem solving.
8. What is the difference between the problem-solving process and the nursing process? How are they similar? Why are they sometimes confused?
9. Describe the common problems that arise during problem solving that impair effectiveness? How can a leader facilitate effective problem solving?

B. Projects/Assignments

1. There has been a great deal of interest recently in the way nurses make clinical decisions. There is also some evidence that nurses and physicians approach clinical problems in different ways. Select a clinical problem commonly faced by both nurses and physicians where you are presently working. Ask at least two nurses and two physicians how they would solve this problem, and compare their responses. You may also want to conduct a literature search at the library for recent articles comparing nurses' and doctors' clinical decision-making strategies.

2. Write a paragraph describing an example of muddy thinking in a leadership or management situation (real or based on a real situation). In a second paragraph, analyze the types of barriers to clear thinking that arose in this situation and, in a third paragraph, describe leadership actions that could remove or at least reduce these barriers. Finally, discuss the potential effect of failing to remove these barriers.

3. Assemble a group of four to five classmates, or nursing staff if available, to discuss a seemingly insoluble problem. If possible, tape the session for later analysis with participants' permission. Identify the steps taken, comparing them with the five steps of problem solving listed in the chapter. Then analyze the session in terms of evidence of any ineffective habits and individual differences in approach to problem solving and how the session could have been more effective, giving specific leadership actions that would facilitate more effective problem solving.

CHAPTER 10
LEADING CHANGE

I. CONTENT OUTLINE

DYNAMICS OF CHANGE
Positive or Negative?
Potential for Change
Characteristics of Change Type
Intensity
Pattern
Pace
Resistance to Change

MANAGING CHANGE
Rational Mode
Assumptions
Diffusion of Innovation
Discussion
Participative Mode
Assumptions
Lewin's Phases of Change
Discussion
Reframing Mode
First-Order Change
Second-Order Change
Reframing

SUMMARY

II. LEARNING OBJECTIVES

After completing this chapter, the reader will be able to:
- Identify the characteristics of a particular planned change.
- Apply the rational approach to change appropriately and effectively.
- Apply the participative approach to change appropriately and effectively.
- Apply the reframing approach to change appropriately and effectively.
- Evaluate the relative strengths and weaknesses of the three approaches to planning and implementing change.

III. NOTE TO INSTRUCTOR

Thinking about change in the abstract may be a challenge for some students, especially those with little previous leadership experience. The use of examples will help them appreciate the applicability of this context to nursing practice and leadership. You can ask the class to suggest some changes they would like to see happen in the clinical setting or in the nursing profession as a whole to use as examples. Then use one of the suggestions to demonstrate how leaders and managers bring about planned change. Using the same example for each of the three types of planned change would also help them see the differences between the rational, participative, and reframing approaches.

The content in this chapter is presented in sequential order, making it easy to follow step by step through the process of change.

STUDENT LEARNING ACTIVITIES

A. Questions for Review and Discussion

1. Is change something you want to encourage or discourage? Why?
2. What types of changes are easiest to implement? Why? What types are hardest? Why?
3. Why do people resist change sometimes?
4. What characteristics of a planned change are likely to create resistance?
5. When is change likely to be welcomed?
6. What are the assumptions underlying the rational approach to change? What type of change is likely to be successfully implemented using the rational approach?
7. List the steps in the rational approach to change. If you were a team leader, what kinds of changes could you implement using this approach? Choose one and describe how you would do this.
8. List the steps in the participative approach to change. If you were a team leader, what kinds of changes could you implement using this approach? Choose one and describe how you would do this.
9. List the steps in the reframing approach to change. If you were a team leader, what kinds of changes could you implement using this approach? Choose one and describe how you would do this.
10. How do the rational, participative, and reframing approaches differ? What are the strengths and limitations of each?

B. Projects/Assignments

1. Select a particular change in health care that you would like to see occur. Describe how you would work through the various phases of each change model to show how it would be used to bring about your selected change. Evaluate the appropriateness and potential effectiveness of each model to the given situation.
2. Describe a change that has occurred to you personally or one you observed closely. Using Lewin's model, analyze the driving and restrained forces in the situation. How did the driving forces overcome the restraining forces?
3. Describe a clinical situation in which the reframing approach might help a patient. Under what circumstances would you recommend this approach? What precautions would be necessary?

4. Write a new version of the Holmes and Hahe stress scale designed especially for students or for staff nurses. List the stressors and assign points to each one. Share your new version with classmates and compare the types of stressors you listed with those your classmates listed.

CHAPTER 11
COMPONENTS OF EFFECTIVE MANAGEMENT

I. CONTENT OUTLINE

II. LEARNING OBJECTIVES

After completing this chapter, the reader will be able to:
* Name the components of effective management.

- Discuss the importance of each component of effective management.
- Evaluate his or her own leadership effectiveness in terms of the components of effective management.
- Evaluate managers in terms of the components of effective management.

III. NOTE TO INSTRUCTOR

As you can see, this chapter parallels Chapter 3, Components of Effective Leadership, in its structure and approach. It is important that students understand not only the difference between leadership and management but also the interrelationship between the two, especially the idea that, to be effective, a manager must be a good leader.

The student is also encouraged to evaluate himself or herself by using the checklist at the end of the chapter. This is especially useful if students have clinical assignments that require them to assume some managerial responsibility. Many RN-BSN students have had some management-oriented employment experience, which they can also evaluate using the checklist.

IV. STUDENT LEARNING ACTIVITIES

A. Questions for Review and Discussion

1. List the seven components of effective management. Define each one and give an example from nursing management; i.e., describe what a nurse manager might do that relates to each of the components.
2. Why is leadership included in the components of effective management?
3. Explain why Mintzberg says managers will tell you they spend their time on one set of activities, yet actually spend most of their time on another set of activities.
4. Compare an ineffective manager with an effective one by describing how each would make staff assignments.
5. What criteria are suggested for use in determining priorities? Explain each one.
6. What should the nurse manager of an inpatient unit monitor daily? Weekly?
7. List at least five different ways to formally monitor unit and staff function.
8. What types of rewards are available to most first-line nurse managers?
9. What are the two schools of thought regarding staff development? Which do you support? Why?
10. Describe a situation in which a nurse manager is expected to represent the staff of his or her unit.
11. Describe a situation in which a nurse manager is expected to represent administration.

B ProjectsAssignments

1. Using the Management Effectiveness Checklist, observe a nurse manager, supervisor, or other management-level individual in a clinical setting. Evaluate this person's effectiveness as a manager, considering ways in which the environment, type of work, and characteristics of the staff impact on this person's effectiveness.

2. Write an essay (one to two pages) on "how *not* to be an effective nurse manager." Share your essay with the class and discuss what each of you consider the worst type of manager you can imagine.

3. Think about the importance of first-line nurse managers in terms of their eventual impact in patient care. In what ways does the effectiveness of the nurse manager impact the quality of care? What are some of the barriers the first-line nurse manager faces when trying to improve the quality of care in his or her unit?

CHAPTER 12
DIRECTING AND ORGANIZING PATIENT CARE

I. CONTENT OUTLINE

Cross-Training
Pros and Cons
Floating
Role of the Manager

SCHEDULING
Centralized Versus Decentralized
Traditional Versus Nontraditional
Flex Time
Self-Scheduling
SpecializationTemporary Personnel
Developing a System

DELEGATION
What You Can and Cannot Delegate
How to Delegate
Role of the Manager

SUMMARY

II. LEARNING OBJECTIVES

After completing this chapter, the reader will be able to:
- Compare and contrast the most commonly used models for organizing nursing care staff.
- Explain the purpose of critical pathways.
- Discuss the impact of staffing decisions on patient outcomes.
- List factors affecting staffing decisions.
- Analyze advantages and disadvantages of various scheduling options.
- Describe scope of responsibility and appropriate assignment for unlicensed assistive personnel.
- Apply the five rights of delegation in the practice setting.
- Discuss the advantages and disadvantages of cross-training and floating.

III. NOTE TO INSTRUCTOR

This is a dense chapter, full of information that relates directly to the practice of nursing leadership and management. Students will learn about the different ways to organize nursing care, staff a unit, schedule staff, and delegate work.

On paper, most of this seems quite simple and straightforward, but in real life, it is not: unbalanced numbers of staff so that only one team will have an experienced LPN; a holiday in the middle of the week when everyone wants that day off; a patient who is so difficult that everyone has requested a "break" from him or her. This is the challenge of nursing management. It requires all of the leadership and management skills learned so far, not just the ones discussed in this chapter. Opportunities to work out such problems in class will better prepare graduates to handle these in the future.

IV. STUDENT LEARNING ACTIVITIES

A. Questions for Review and Discussion

1. Compare and contrast case, functional, team, and primary nursing care management and patient-focused care.
2. Describe how each model is used to organize the delivery of nursing care on inpatient units and in home health.
3. On the blackboard, under each of these models, list their advantages and disadvantages. Try to add to what is mentioned in the chapter.
4. Which model do you think most patients would prefer? Why?
5. Which model do you think most nurses prefer? Why?
6. What is a DRG? How do DRGs affect staffing decisions?
7. What is meant by the term "patient acuity"? Should this term be defined in the same way for acute and long-term care settings? Why or why not?
8. Distinguish between productive and nonproductive time. Can nonproductive time be eliminated altogether?
9. What are the factors that must be considered in deciding how many staff members are needed for an inpatient unit?
10. What do the initials RN, LPN, and UAP stand for? What is the difference in educational preparation of these three levels of staff? How does each contribute to patient care?
11. What are some of the concerns raised about the use of UAPs?
12. On what basis should a nurse manager decide which tasks can be delegated to a UAP?
13. Explain cross-training. Why is it currently an issue in nursing? What are the advantages and disadvantages of cross-training nursing staff?
14. Why is floating often a source of concern for nursing staff? For nurse managers?
15. Describe an effective way to "float" staff in an emergency. Should "floating" be a routine procedure? Why or why not?
16. Explain the difference between centralized and decentralized staffing. What are the advantages and disadvantages of each?
17. What is flex time? When is it appropriate?
18. What is self-scheduling? What are the advantages and disadvantages?
19. What must a nurse manager know to be able to delegate work safely?
20. What are the five "rights" of delegation? Explain each one and give an example of how they affect the way a nurse manager would assign work to a UAP.

B. Projects/Assignments

1. Draw a table that lists the advantages and disadvantages of each model for delivering nursing care. Discuss the relative importance of each of these and decide which one best suits your philosophy of nursing care and which best suits the organization in which you are working.
2. Look at the staffing model used on the unit or team to which you have been assigned for clinical experience. List the number of RNs, LPNs, and UAPs available on one midweek shift. Then describe a typical patient census: numbers of patients, diagnoses, and major needs for nursing care. With your classmates, discuss the various ways in which you can assign available staff to patient care responsibilities. What are the most difficult decisions to make? Are resources

adequate to provide quality care? Is there a better way to organize and deploy existing staff?

3. Form a "nursing team" with four or five of your classmates and try to create a work schedule for the next month. Assume that you, as a group, are the only staff with sufficient preparation to serve as charge nurses. How can you cover all three shifts 7 days a week adequately? Analyze the decision-making process that occurred: What were your most difficult decisions? What were the easiest? How did the group finally resolve the difficult issues? Is the group satisfied with the outcome (resulting schedule)? Why or why not?

4. Contact your State Nurses Association and/or Board of Nursing for information on the preparation of UAPs in your state. What, if any, educational preparation is required? What are they allowed by law to do? What are they not allowed to do?

5. Using information about the patients or clients served by your assigned agency or unit, devise an ideal assignment plan. Be sure that assignments are both appropriate and fair and that their outcomes would promote both the efficiency and effectiveness of the caregiver.

CHAPTER 13
INDIVIDUAL EVALUATION
PROCEDURES

I. CONTENT OUTLINE

INFORMAL INDIVIDUAL EVALUATION
Purpose of Providing Evaluative Feedback
Guidelines for Providing Constructive Feedback
Provide Both Positive and Negative Feedback
Give Immediate Feedback
Provide Frequent Feedback
Be Specific
Be Objective
Base on Observable Behavior
Communicate Appropriately
Include Suggestions for Change
Seeking Evaluative Feedback
When Evaluative Feedback Is Needed
Responding to Evaluative Feedback

FORMAL INDIVIDUAL EVALUATION
Purpose of Formal Evaluation
Accountability
Administrative Intervention
Rewards
Identification of Educational Needs
Performance Appraisals
Setting Objectives and Standards
Using Objectives
Essentials of Management by Objectives
Using Job Descriptions and Standards
Implementing the Plan
Evaluating Outcomes
Ensuring Fair, Uniform Procedures
Peer Review
Fundamentals of Peer Review
Uses of Peer Review Data
Evaluating the Marginal Staff Member
Excuses for Inaction
Importance of Intervention
Factors Leading to Marginal Performance
Resolution of the Problem

Fear of Firing
SUMMARY

II. LEARNING OBJECTIVES

After completing this chapter, the reader will be able to:
- Provide both positive and negative feedback in a constructive manner.
- Write objectives that are appropriate and include observable outcomes.
- Define management by objectives and list its advantages and disadvantages.
- Conduct a formal performance appraisal.
- Evaluate the objectivity and constructiveness of evaluation procedures.
- Participate in peer review procedures.

III. NOTE TO INSTRUCTOR

Basic concepts are presented in the first part of this chapter and should be considered the foundation for the second part, in which formal evaluation procedures are discussed. Most students have been evaluated before, but many have not had experience evaluating other people, which is often a difficult process. Those who have never reprimanded or terminated an employee may not realize how difficult this is for most managers. In fact, managers often go to great lengths to avoid doing this. You may find that it is much easier for these students to relate to the distress of the reprimanded or terminated employee.

Providing feedback to one another through classroom practice must be handled carefully but is truly a valuable experience for most students. Some suggestions for doing this follow in the Student Learning Activities section.

IV. STUDENT LEARNING ACTIVITIES

A. Questions for Review and Discussion

1. Why is feedback so important? What happens when employees receive little or no feedback?
2. Why do experienced staff need feedback? What is the difference between constructive and destructive feedback?
3. What are the nine characteristics of constructive feedback? Explain each one.
4. Why is it important to ask for feedback? Under what circumstances would you do this?
5. If the evaluative feedback you receive is negative, how should you respond?
6. Why is the provision of formal evaluation an important part of effective management? What is the purpose of it?
7. What is a performance appraisal?
8. What is MBO? How can objectives be used in formal evaluation?
9. Describe the process by which a staff nurse would be evaluated, using objectives set by the nurse manager 6 months before.
10. What is the purpose of a job description? When would you write your own job description? How would you go about doing this?
11. What is the difference between peer review and management review? Which is most common? Why?

B. Projects/Assignments

1. Write five different sentences a leader could use to tell a staff member that he or she has very good interpersonal (communication) skills but needs to improve technical skills related to IV therapy. Evaluate each version: Which one is best? Why?

2. Write a job description for a newly created school health nurse position in a small rural school district that will have only one nurse for the entire district.

3. Role-play the evaluation of a staff nurse who has had a very high rate of absenteeism for the last 6 weeks. The nurse is also late several times a week and fails to complete paperwork before leaving in the evening. Ask class members to observe and critique your evaluative session, reminding them to observe the roles for providing constructive feedback.

4. With another colleague or classmate, role-play a performance appraisal session in which the staff member has failed to achieve all but one of the objectives that had been mutually agreed on 6 months ago. Evaluate the nurse-manager's actions in terms of effective communication, the components of effective management, and adherence to the guidelines for providing feedback. Then evaluate the staff member in terms of effective communication skills, the components of effective leadership, and guidelines for receiving feedback. You may have to refer to earlier chapters for some of these guidelines. If time permits, switch roles and repeat the session.

CHAPTER 14
MANAGING A BUDGET

I. CONTENT OUTLINE

IMPORTANCE OF FINANCIAL MANAGEMENT
Effect on People's Work
Planning the Budget
Planning
Roles, Responsibilities, and Authority

RESPONSIBILITY FOR FINANCIAL MANAGEMENT
Chief Executive Officer (CEO)
Governing Board
Chief Financial Officer (CFO)
Managers

TYPES OF BUDGET
Incremental Budgeting
Zero-Base Budgeting

THE BUDGET PROCESS
Phase I. Planning
Phase II. Drafting
Phase III. Modification and Approval
Phase IV. Monitoring

SUMMARY

II. LEARNING OBJECTIVES

After completing this chapter, the reader will be able to:
- Explain why financial management is important to the nurse manager.
- Identify the individuals within an organization who have responsibility for budget preparation, approval and monitoring.
- Distinguish zero-based budgeting from incremental budgeting.
- Read and explain a simple budget variance report for a nursing unit.
- Understand the factors that influence productivity at the unit level.

III. NOTE TO INSTRUCTOR

This is not an easy chapter to master. Students may need to be cautioned to read it carefully, especially the second half, which contains a number of formulas and calculations. None of these are very complex; it simply takes some time and thought to follow the reasoning presented and to learn how the calculations are done. In addition, the formulas build one upon the other, so that the student who tries to rush through the first few is in danger of becoming lost when working through the later ones. Reviewing the material in class and asking students to calculate such things as FTEs and shift differentials given different cost figures will help students become thoroughly familiar and comfortable with this material.

IV. STUDENT LEARNING ACTIVITIES

A. Questions for Review and Discussion

1. What interest does a staff nurse have in a budgeting process? How would he or she be affected by it?
2. What is "planning the budget"? Why should a nursing staff and nurse manager be alert for this occurring?
3. What is the relationship between planning and budgeting? Why should they be done together?
4. What is the responsibility of each of the following in the budgeting process using a participative approach?
   CEO
   CFO
   Nurse Manager
   Staff Member
   Board of Trustees
5. What is the difference between zero-based budgeting and incremental budgeting? Which is more common? Which requires more analysis of every expense?
6. What is the difference between income and expense? Give examples of each that would occur in an inpatient medical unit?
7. Why are nurse managers asked to complete monthly budget reports? What is typically involved in preparing one?
8. What is a budget variance? Is a variance always negative? Why or why not?
9. How are hours per patient-day (HPPD) calculated? Give an example.
10. What is an FTE? How is it calculated?
11. How does a nurse manager estimate the number of FTEs needed to staff a unit?
12. What is the difference between hours worked and hours paid? Why does this occur?
13. What is a shift differential? How is it calculated? Give examples.
14. Explain why having completed and obtained approval for a unit budget is not the end of a budgeting process. What comes next? Why?

B. Projects/Assignments

1. Ask permission to photocopy an annual operating budget for a nursing care unit or small community health agency. (The budget should not include individual names on salary figures to protect confidentiality.) Compare the budgeted distribution of available funds to the organization's goals. Then try to work out a different distribution assuming 20 percent more available funds and 20 percent less available. Analyze the effect each would have on the quality of the nursing care given.

2. Role-play a budget meeting between the nurse manager of a cardiac care unit and the CFO. The CFO has asked the nurse manager to either reduce the unit budget by 10 percent across the board or to fire one staff member on each shift (days-evenings-nights) in order to make up for a serious budget shortage experienced by the organization.

3. A grateful former patient has given a $10,000 gift to your home health agency, specifying that the gift be used in whatever way your home health team decides. (It was your team that took care of the posthospitalization.) Conduct a mock team meeting led by the RN team leader to decide how to spend the gift. There are no restrictions on the gift except that the expenditures must be legal and ethical. Six team members include: team leader RN, staff RN, LPN, and three HHAs.

CHAPTER 15
INFORMATICS AND
NURSING MANAGEMENT

I. CONTENT OUTLINE

INFORMATICS
Nursing Informatics
Databases and Data Sets
Nursing Nomenclature and Taxonomies
North American Nursing Diagnosis Association (NANDA)
Omaha System
Home Health Care Classification
Nursing Interventions Classification
CHARACTERISTICS OF SUCCESSFUL SYSTEMS
NURSING INFORMATICS AND NURSING MANAGEMENT
Computer-Based Patient Record (CPR)
Benefits
Caregiver Resistance
Management Applications
Department Planning Activities
Security Issues
Audit Trails
TELEHEALTH
SUMMARY

II. LEARNING OBJECTIVES

After completing this chapter, the reader will be able to:
- List the components of successful nursing information systems.
- Describe existing nursing nomenclatures and taxonomies.
- Discuss the advantages and disadvantages of implementing computer-based patient record systems.
- Outline the use of technology in nursing management.
- Discuss the function and future of telehealth.

III. NOTE TO INSTRUCTOR

The contribution of informatics to nursing practice and nursing management is an exciting one. The possibilities for more efficient sharing and evaluation of data are endless. The advances are coming so quickly, however, that it is virtually impossible to keep information on either hardware or software up-to-the minute. As a consequence, this chapter will probably need supplementation with journal articles and with new information on how our colleagues are using informatics today, and how they plan to use informatics in the future. Students would also benefit from opportunities to use new software and to participate in telehealth.

IV. STUDENT LEARNING ACTIVITIES

A. Questions for Review and Discussion

1. Define the term informatics. What do the terms health informatics and nursing informatics mean?
2. List six or seven ways in which informatics contributes to nursing practice and/or management.
3. How can patient outcome data be used to improve the delivery of nursing care? What precautions need to be observed in doing this?
4. What is NMDS? What variables are included? What is its purpose?
5. Name the four most common nursing classification systems and describe each one.
6. What conditions need to be in place for a nursing information system to be successful?
7. What are the advantages of an electronic patient record? Disadvantages?
8. How can informatics be used to support planning?
9. What are some of the security issues associated with the use of electronic records and databases? How can security be protected?
10. What is telehealth? What are the most important management issues related to telehealth? Professional issues?

B. Projects/Assignments

1. Interview the individual in charge of the management information systems in the facility where you work or are assigned for clinical experience. Ask him or her how information is obtained, entered into the system, analyzed, and reported. Be sure to ask how the security of the system is assured and the cost of these systems, both installation and maintenance.
2. To further explore the use of electronic patient and administrative data in health care, interview first-line nurse managers and staff nurses. Ask them the same questions as in #1. Also ask them how electronic data is helpful and/or not helpful to them.
3. Do a literature search on the subject of telehealth. What new applications did you find? How many of them are associated with nursing care? What are some of the advantages described? What concerns are raised?
4. If possible, take advantage of an opportunity to attend a professional conference in your locality. Talk with the vendors of software and hardware designed to support patient and administrative information systems. Carefully evaluate the degree to which these systems provide real advantages over paper-based systems. Are they worth the cost and the effort involved? Alternatively, search for this information online and answer the same questions.

5. Do an online search for software that supports planning. How much did you find? How many were specific to health care? How could they be useful to nurse managers?

CHAPTER 16
PROJECT PLANNING AND
EVALUATION

I. CONTENT OUTLINE

PLANNING
Types of Planning
Involvement in Planning
Impetus for Planning

STAGES OF PROJECT PLANNING
Stage I. Preparation
Phase 1. Conceptual Development
Phase 2. Detailed Plan
Phase 3. Approval
Stage II. Action
Phase 4. Implementation
Phase 5. Monitoring Implementation
Stage III. Completion
Phase 6. Evaluation of Outcomes
Phase 7. Institutionalization or Termination

SUMMARY

II. LEARNING OBJECTIVES

After completing this chapter, the reader will be able to:
List and explain the three stages of planning.
- Outline a plan for a health-related project.
- Identify situational variables that would affect a project plan.
- Suggest ways to generate creative alternative approaches.
- Use a simple rating system to evaluate alternative solutions.
- Present a project plan in a persuasive manner.
- Use a Gantt or similar chart to monitor implementation.

III. NOTE TO INSTRUCTOR

It is easy to get lost in the detail of this chapter. To prevent this, you might want to suggest that students review the chapter outline at the beginning of the chapter and read the summary at the end before reading the chapter itself. Keeping a copy of Box 16–1 on hand or marking the page so they can refer back to it periodically to see where they are in the planning process should also help.

You can work through several real or imaginary projects with the class as a whole to help them see the importance of the many steps and the sequence of events needed to accomplish thorough planning. The chapter itself also has plenty of examples that should help the reader understand how this information is applied in real life.

There are a great number of acronyms in this chapter. You might want to list them and ask the class if they can identify and explain each one after reading the chapter.

IV. STUDENT LEARNING ACTIVITIES

A. Questions for Review and Discussion

1. What are the differences between project planning, strategic planning, and health care planning? Give an example of each.
2. Name the three stages of the project planning process. Then list the seven phases under their respective stages.
3. What is the primary difference between reactive and proactive planning? Why is this difference important to managers?
4. What is a breakpoint? Give an example from health care.
5. What is a performance gap? Give two or three examples of performance gaps a nurse manager might identify on his or her unit.
6. Why is the identification of specific objectives delayed until Phase 2?
7. What is a stakeholder? Identify the stakeholders in the School of Nursing example (found in the Involvement in Planning section of Chapter 16).
8. Use the spinal cord treatment example from Chapter 16 or an example of your own to show how the following assessment frameworks can be used in project planning:
   a. Systems-based framework
   b. Service-oriented Framework
   c. Fishbone framework
   d. Affinity map and relationship diagram
9. Why does a project need a sponsor? A champion?
10. What is the difference between brainstorming and the nominal group technique? How would a nurse leader or manager decide which to use to generate ideas?
11. Define Synectics and describe how it can be used in project planning.
12. What is idealized redesign? How can it be used in planning?
13. Once ideas have been generated, what are the three formal approaches to selecting the best one as described in this chapter? Explain each one, including its pros and cons.
14. What is SMART? How is it useful to project planning?
15. Write three objectives for an organization-wide planning project.
16. Describe the techniques a nurse can use to persuade the sponsor to approve a proposed project.
17. What do the initials WBS stand for? Why is WBS used in planning?
18. What do the initials WIIFM stand for? Why should you keep this in mind while planning?

19. Why is it important for the nurse manager to identify and obtain the resources needed to carry out a project? How is this done?
20. What is the difference between GANTT, PERT, and Critical Path charts?
21. Why would a planner use most optimistic, most likely, and most pessimistic estimates?
22. What is formative evaluation? How is it done? Why is it used in planning?
23. Describe Phases 6 and 7 of project planning. Why are they important?

B. Projects/Assignments

1. With a small group of colleagues or classmates, try using brainstorming and/or the nominal group technique to identify a health care delivery problem and to devise three to five alternative strategies for improving health care delivery in a given situation. Subject each of the alternatives to the scenario and simulation approaches to evaluation. Critique the value of each approach in helping the group select one of the alternatives.
2. Write a set of three to five objectives for the pediatric playroom project. Ask five or six members of the class to share their lists of objectives with the class. Critique the objectives using the SMART criteria.
3. Create a WBS, Gantt chart, and Critical Path chart for the pediatric playroom project.
4. Interview a nurse manager who is responsible for managing at least one inpatient unit or several teams of home care workers. Ask the nurse manager if he or she does any planning. If so, what type of planning and how useful has it been? If not, why not? Finally, ask the nurse manager what the most difficult aspects of planning are and how valuable he or she thinks planning is.
5. Using either the Case Study scenario (developing a new Research Center) from Chapter 16 or one of your own, describe how you would proceed through all of the stages, phases, and individual steps (see Box 16–1) of project planning to complete this health care-related project. Include a statement of purpose, assessment worksheet, desired outcomes, alternative ways to implement the project (with pros and cons for each alternative), specific objectives, WBS, and Gantt or PERT chart. Describe the issues involved in the implementation and evaluation of the project itself.

CHAPTER 17
ORGANIZATIONAL DYNAMICS

I. CONTENT OUTLINE

HEALTH CARE ORGANIZATIONS

ORGANIZATIONS AS COMPLEX OPEN SYSTEMS
Wholeness
Individuality
Hierarchy
Complexity
Openness
Patterns and Growth

ORGANIZATIONAL STRUCTURE
The Bureaucracy
Traditional Structural Design
Matrix or Organic Design
Variations in Designs
Medical Staff
Board of Trustees
Nurses

ORGANIZATIONAL OPERATIONS
Formal and Informal Goals
Formal and Informal Operations
Breaks in Communication
Relationship Games

PATTERNS OF RELATIONSHIPS IN ORGANIZATIONS
Distribution of Power and Authority
Challenging the Traditional Distribution of Authority

SUMMARY

II. LEARNING OBJECTIVES

After completing this chapter, the reader will be able to:
- Differentiate the various types of health care organizations.
- Describe the characteristics of health care organizations as complex, open systems.
- Compare the structure and function of a bureaucratic structure and an organic one.
- Address both the formal and informal levels of operation.
- Differentiate authority, accountability and responsibility.
- Identify the patterns of relationships found in organizations.

III. NOTE TO INSTRUCTOR

Far too many practicing nurses ignore the "big picture" aspects of the organization in which they work. Yet they are all affected by the structure and function of these organizations. For those who have difficulty moving from the micro (individual) to macro (larger systems) level of thinking, it may be helpful to begin with a discussion of the differences they've noticed in the various clinical agencies to which they have been assigned and/or employed. This may help them think of organizations as whole systems. The examples in the chapter should also help them accomplish this shift in perspective.

IV. STUDENT LEARNING ACTIVITIES

A. Questions for Review and Discussion

1. In what types of organizations do nurses usually work?
2. How different do you think it would be to work in a health care organization as opposed to a non-health care organization?
3. How can you identify and describe the culture or "personality" of an entire organization? Give an example.
4. Why is the work climate of an organization important to nurse leaders and managers?
5. What is a hierarchy? Describe a traditional nursing hierarchy.
6. Describe the complete life cycle of an organization.
7. What is a bureaucracy? List the four major characteristics of a bureaucratic organization. In what ways is bureaucracy helpful? In what ways is it a problem?
8. Define strategic apex, operational core, middle management, support staff, and technical staff. What does each of these groups of people do in an organization? Why are they needed? How do they relate to each other? Which of these components are usually found in a new, small organization?
9. What is a matrix organizational structure? Compare and contrast the five designs illustrated in Figure 17–6 in your own words. What are the advantages and disadvantages of each? In which one do you think you would prefer to work?
10. What is the function of a hospital Board of Trustees? How do the decisions they make affect staff nurses and patient care?
11. Describe the relationship of the medical staff to the rest of an acute care facility's staff. How is this changing?
12. What is a hospitalist? An intensivist? What is the staff nurse's position in the power structure of most acute care facilities? Who has less power and authority? Who has more?
13. What is the difference between the formal and informal goals of an organization? Give three or four examples of common operational goals of a health care organization. How does each one affect staff nurses and patient care delivery? What is the "shadow organization"?
14. What is meant by the phrase "proper channels of communication"? What is the "grapevine"? How does it operate? What are the advantages and disadvantages of having an active grapevine in an organization?
15. Describe the game playing that can occur in a health care organization. How does it affect people who work in these organizations?

16. Explain the relationships between accountability, authority and responsibility.
17. Explain "shared governance" and describe how it can affect the power structure of a health care organization.

B. Projects/Assignments

1. Obtain a copy of your organization's (or clinical agency's) Table of Organization. Using this as a model for the formal level of operation, observe how decisions are made and redraw the Table of Organization to represent the informal level of operation. The same can be done with the organization's stated goals and the informal goals.
2. Create a new (original) organizational design in diagram form. Write a description of how the various parts or components would interact, how your design is superior to existing design, and what disadvantages it might have.
3. Write descriptions of your first impressions of two different health care organizations as shown in the section on wholeness in Chapter 17. Compare and contrast the two descriptions and suggest simple changes each organization could make to improve the impression they make on first-time visitors.
4. Write a scenario, either from real life or an imaginary one, that describes how a first-line nurse manager or staff nurse can get caught up in the Karpman Triangle. Then suggest ways in which the manager and individual staff members can change their behavior to get out of the triangle.

CHAPTER 18
WORKPLACE HEALTH AND SAFETY

I. CONTENT OUTLINE

II. LEARNING OBJECTIVES

After completing this chapter, the reader will be able to:
- Identify the most common risks to employee health and safety in health care settings.
- Suggest strategies for reducing health and safety risks in health care settings.
- Distinguish employee and employer responsibilities for workplace health and safety.
- Outline the process for designing risk reduction programs.
- Discuss redesign of the social and technical environment in health care organizations.

II. NOTE TO THE INSTRUCTOR

No workplace is entirely free of health and safety risks, but it may surprise students that health care settings have a relatively high level of risk and a wide range of sources of these risks. The purpose of this chapter is not to frighten readers but to alert them so that they can take preventive action for themselves and for others.

Many of the topics introduced in this chapter are issues of current concern to the profession. There is a great deal of new information coming out as the research and debates continue. For this reason, the use of supplementary material from current journals, professional organizations, and regulatory bodies will be especially helpful when presenting this material.

III. STUDENT LEARNING ACTIVITIES

A. Questions for Review and Discussion

1. Why is the subject of workplace health and safety of concern to nurse managers?
2. To what types of workplace health and safety risks are nurses exposed?
3. What types of violence are health care workers exposed to? List the "rules" for personal safety in community-based nursing.
4. What action is suggested when faced with an angry or hostile coworker?
5. What should you do if you receive a threatening telephone call at work?
6. Why is substance misuse among nurses a serious concern?
7. What is the best way to handle a suspicion that a coworker may be involved in serious substance misuse?
8. What types of work conditions lead to job-related stress? What are the warning signs of job-related-stress?
9. Whose responsibility is it to achieve stress reduction in the workplace?
10. Why are needlestick hazards a current concern of professional nursing organizations?
11. What is the appropriate response when an accidental needlestick occurs?
12. Why has latex sensitivity increased? What type of assistance do sensitized employees need?
13. What is the most common physical injury experienced by LPNs and nursing assistants? How can a nurse manager help staff avoid physical injury at work?
14. Describe the process by of developing and implementing a risk reduction program. Whose responsibility is it to see that this is done?
15. Explain the difference between a supportive and nonsupportive work environment. Give an example of each.
16. Explain the difference between an empowering and an alienating environment. Give an example of each.
17. Define job redesign. What type of redesign could be done within a nursing unit?
18. Give three or four examples of changes in the physical environment of a nursing unit that would reduce steps and increase patient safety and comfort.

B. Projects/Assignments

1. Investigate the laws and regulations concerning impaired nurses in your state. Interview several employers and staff nurses to determine their knowledge of these rules and opinions regarding their fairness and effectiveness, particularly

the degree to which they provide safeguards for the patient, the employee, and the employer.

2. Evaluate the extent to which your assigned unit or agency promotes staff development. Suggest ways in which staff development could be promoted and estimate the relative cost and benefits of your suggestions.

3. Conduct an informal survey of health and safety hazards that exist in your assigned unit. To what extent are patients and employees well protected? What additional actions could be taken by management to reduce these risks? Why do you think they have not been done yet?

4. Search the last 6 months' issues of *American Nurse* (published by the ANA). How many health and safety issues are mentioned? What steps can a professional organization take to protect the health and safety of individual nurses?

CHAPTER 19
QUALITY IMPROVEMENT

I. CONTENT OUTLINE

QUALITY DEFINED

GOALS OF QUALITY IMPROVEMENT

CONTINUOUS QUALITY IMPROVEMENT

TOTAL QUALITY MANAGEMENT

ASPECTS OF HEALTH CARE TO EVALUATE
Structure
Process
Outcome
Nursing Management Minimum Data Set

DATA COLLECTION PROCEDURES
Record Audits
Observation
Interviews and Questionnaires
Focus Groups

QUALITY IMPROVEMENT AT THE UNIT LEVEL
Scope
Standards
Indicators and Criteria

QUALITY IMPROVEMENT AT THE ORGANIZATION LEVEL
Quality Circles
Continuous Quality Improvement
Example

ISSUES RELATED TO CQI AND TQM

SUMMARY

II. LEARNING OBJECTIVES

After completing this chapter, the reader will be able to:
- Discuss the similarities and differences among quality assurance, quality improvement, continuous quality improvement, and total quality improvement.
- Distinguish structure, process, and outcome variables in formal evaluation procedures.
- Participate in the development and implementation of a continuous quality improvement program at the unit level.

- Participate in the implementation of total quality management within a health care organization.

III. NOTE TO INSTRUCTOR

Quality improvement (QI) is a well-established responsibility of any health care organization. Involvement in QI is virtually a certainty at some point in every nurse's career. For nurse managers, familiarity with these procedures is no longer optional but an expectation of most employees. If possible, every student should have the opportunity to participate in the QI procedures of the agency where he or she has been assigned. Seeing how it works in real life will add the hands-on dimension a textbook cannot supply.

IV. STUDENT LEARNING ACTIVITIES

A. Questions for Review and Discussion

1. What is the difference among QA, QI, CQI and TQM? Define each term and show how they differ.
2. What is a benchmark? How does it relate to quality improvement (QI)?
3. Define "quality" in your own words. Explain the difference between retrospective, concurrent, and prospective types of QI.
4. What are the four basic elements of CQI? Give an example of each.
5. What are Donabedian's three classic dimensions included in a complete evaluation of health care services? Give several (at least 2 or 3) examples of each.
6. Explain the differences among independent, dependent, and interdependent nursing functions.
7. What is the Nursing Management Minimum Data Set (NMMDS)? How does it relate to QI? What variables are included in the NMMDS?
8. What is a record audit? How is it done? For what purpose?
9. Define scope, standards of care, indicators and criteria in terms of QI. Give an example of each related to a common clinical problem.
10. Whose responsibility is it to establish QI procedures across the institution? How should staff nurses and nurse managers be involved?
10. What is a quality circle? What are the pros and cons of using quality circles in a health care organization?
12. Describe the process by which a unit level QI project would be initiated and completed.
13. What are some of the most common obstacles to implementing TQM? How can they be overcome?

B. Projects/Assignments

1. Select a common nursing problem such as fever or nausea to study as a group. Next, identify a specific patient population that frequently experiences this problem. Then, work through the steps leading to a set of quality improvement guidelines for this problem: defining the scope and important aspects of the problem, developing a standard of care, and, finally, identifying the indicators and related criteria. How difficult was it to find indicators and related

criteria? How difficult was it to find all additional information about each of these? Is there sufficient nursing research on the subject? How did you decide where to set the thresholds? What did you learn about the problem? What did you learn about quality improvement?

2. Review the 16 variables contained within the NMMDS. Describe how you would gather data in each of these categories in an acute care setting and in a home health agency. Which of these variables do you think would especially impact on the quality of care given? Why?

3. Ask for a copy of a recently completed QI project at the facility where you work and/or to which you are assigned for clinical experience. Compose this report with the format suggested in Chapter 19. How do they differ? How are they alike? Which format do you think is preferable? Why? Have you seen any evidence that the results of the QI project were used to make improvements in patient care at the facility? Estimate the amount of time spent on completing the project and compare to the impact on patient care. Was the time well spent? If not, how would you, as a first-line nurse manager, improve the payoff from QI efforts?

CHAPTER 20
WORKPLACE ETHICS

I. CONTENT OUTLINE

ETHICS, MORALS, AND VALUES
Values
Morals
Ethics

BASIS FOR MAKING ETHICAL DECISIONS
Core Values
Beneficence
General Principles

ETHICAL DILEMMAS
Interpersonal Dilemmas
Intrapersonal Dilemmas

ETHICAL ISSUES OF THE WORKPLACE
Levels of Interaction
Types of Issues
Organizational Issues
System-Wide Issues

ETHICAL DECISION MAKING
Acting in Accord with Your Principles
Resolving Ethical Dilemmas
Management Role

SUMMARY

II. LEARNING OBJECTIVES

After completing this chapter, the reader will be able to:
- Define personal and professional values, morals, and ethics.
- Explain the ethical principle(s) on which decisions in the workplace are made.
- Identify the common ethical issues that arise in the workplace, particularly in health care settings.
- Apply personal and professional values and ethical principles in resolution of ethical dilemmas.
- Discuss the nurse manager's role in supporting ethical practice.

III. NOTE TO THE INSTRUCTOR

This is an entirely new chapter written for the fourth edition. Some of the information that is typically found in nursing ethics chapters and articles will not be found here because, to the extent possible, the chapter focuses only on work-related issues, not the patient-care issues usually addressed in nursing textbooks.

Students who enjoy discussion and debate will like this chapter. Those who want clear-cut answers, however, may have more difficulty with it and need help in understanding that there are no easy answers to many ethics questions.

Attention should also be directed to the Code for Nurses, an important document for all practicing nurses, and to the guidelines for accepting or rejecting an assignment. Both should be useful to them after graduation. Both are dynamic, living documents: New versions of these documents may be published after this book goes to print. Instructors should look for them in the future.

IV. STUDENT LEARNING ACTIVITIES

A. Questions for Review and Discussion

1. Define the terms ethics, morals, and values. What is the difference between ethics and morals? Ethics and values?
2. What kinds of values and ethics questions are likely to arise in a health care setting? Distinguish between patient care and leadership and management issues.
3. Describe the Code for Nurses. What is its purpose? What issues are addressed in the Code? What issues are not addressed?
4. What is the "sacred" ethical principle of health care that Flarey refers to? What does it mean? What is the opposite of this "sacred" principle?
5. List the eight core values mentioned in the chapter. Relate each one to the work setting.
6. What is the difference between an interpersonal and intrapersonal dilemma? Give an example of each.
7. Distinguish between intraorganizational, interorganizational, and health care system–level ethical issues. Give an example of each.
8. What are some of the most common workplace ethical issues? Which one have you encountered at work or during clinical experience?
9. Review Solomon's "seven deadly sins" of managers. Which have you observed? Which do you think occurs most often in nursing management?
10. Review the guidelines for accepting and rejecting an assignment. What are the basic principles underlying the guidelines? Be sure you make a distinction between legal and ethical issues.
11. Discuss the Tavistock Group's five principles guiding the delivery of health care. Identify the current issues and abstracts in health care delivery that they address. How would you modify the principles if you had the opportunity?
12. Describe the process for resolving an ethical dilemma. Show how the process can be applied to an ethical dilemma that arises in a work situation.
13. What can a manager do to support ethical behavior? List specific actions and describe the responsibility of administration, managers, and individual employees in taking each of these actions.

B. Projects/Assignments

1. Search the professional literature and media for a description of an ethical issue related to nursing (be sure it is one that involves nurses, not just other disciplines). Critically analyze the issues in terms of the principles discussed in Chapter 20. How would you act if you were personally involved? How do you think the issue will be resolved?

2. Write a fictional but reality-based scenario in which a nurse manager discovers that an experienced staff nurse has been documenting care that was not given. Then describe how the manager could work through the process of resolving this ethical dilemma. Identify the principles that you would use to make your decision if you were the nurse manager. Do you think most nurses would make the same decision? Why or why not?

3. Interview at least five people using the list of six unethical actions that Greengard found were common in the workplace. Ask them which they have observed in the last year and how often, and what they did when they saw it happening.

4. Take each of the "seven deadly sins" that Solomon says managers commit and write a paragraph describing an instance in which you observed the "sin" being committed. Critically analyze each situation. Why did this occur? How could it be prevented?

CHAPTER 21
POWER, EMPOWERMENT, AND
POLITICAL INFLUENCE

I. CONTENT OUTLINE

Contract Administration
Grievances
Binding Arbitration
Collective Bargaining from a Management Viewpoint
Preventing Unionization
Supervision and Management under a Collective Bargaining Contract
Handling Grievances
POWER AND POLITICS IN THE COMMUNITY
Power Distribution in the Community
Political Action: Influencing the Flow of Power and Decision Making
Entering the Decision-Making Channel
The Agenda or Desired Change
Identifying the People for and against Change
Barriers to Effective Implementation
SUMMARY

II. LEARNING OBJECTIVES

After completing this chapter, the reader will be able to:
- Define power, empowerment, politics, and influence.
- Discuss the issues involved in empowering employees.
- Identify the sources of power in a given situation.
- Describe the distribution of power within an organization and in the community.
- Use power strategies to bring about change.
- Debate the advantages and disadvantages of collective bargaining from both labor's and management's point of view.
- Describe the activities of labor and management during the development of a collective bargaining agreement.
- Compare and contrast the rights and responsibilities of labor and management in a grievance procedure.
- Participate in political action to bring about change.

III. NOTE TO INSTRUCTOR

This is a long but interesting chapter that addresses some lively and controversial topics. You can encourage students to think about and discuss their own attitudes toward the use of power and of collective bargaining in the nursing profession. Inviting speakers from the district nurses' association and/or local bargaining units that represent nurses would enliven this discussion. Some caution may be advisable here. At times, these issues become so heated in a given locale that even mentioning them brings criticism from local administrators and facilities. It is wise to handle this material with sensitivity to the strong feelings on each side.

IV. STUDENT LEARNING ACTIVITIES

A. Questions for Review and Discussion

1. Define *power.*
2. List the 10 sources of power and give an example of each related to health care.

3. What is the difference between overt and covert uses of power?
4. How is power usually distributed in an organization?
5. When is it appropriate to use a power-based strategy for change? What are some of the precautions one should consider before using them?
6. Describe the six steps in using a power-based approach to bringing about change. Give an example at each step.
7. Define collective bargaining.
8. What are the pros and cons of nurses' involvement in collective bargaining?
9. What is an organizing council?
10. Describe how an election takes place and a contract is negotiated.
11. Define mediation, fact-finding, and binding arbitration. How are they similar? How are they different?
12. What are the pros and cons of work stoppages from an employee's point of view? From a manager's point of view?
13. What is a grievance? Give several examples.
14. Describe how a grievance is usually handled under a collective bargaining agreement.
15. What steps can management take to prevent unionization? Why would they want to do this?
16. Once a collective bargaining contract is in place, what is important for first-line managers to know?
17. Why is collective bargaining such a controversial issue in nursing?
18. What and who are influentials, effectors, and activists in regard to community-wide power and influence?
19. How does each of these groups impact on community-wide decision making?
20. Compare and contrast the high-initiative and low-initiative patterns of political activism.
21. Describe how decision making occurs in the community using the Bachrach and Baratz-based diagram as your framework (Figure 21–1).
22. List the four barriers to effective implementation from the Bachrach and Baratz-based model and give examples of each.
23. Discuss nurses' roles in influencing community-based decision making on health-related issues. Is this an important role for nurses? Why or why not?

B. Projects/Assignments

1. Using newspaper accounts and local informants, trace the progress of an important health-related issue in your community. Using the Bachrach and Baratz-based form of decision making (Figure 21–1), identify the forces for and against change, the decision-making channels, the barriers to change in the decision-making arena, and the degree to which the change was implemented. Analyze the outcome in terms of actions that could have taken place to either promote or prevent it.
2. Set up a debate on the pros and cons of collective bargaining. Create two teams of five each to play the roles of a) staff nurse, b) nursing administrator, c) first-line manager, d) nursing assistant, e) CEO. Each should speak from the viewpoint of his or her assigned role. Allow time for each team to present their argument (3 minutes apiece) and then 1 minute each for rebuttal. Ask the class to vote on which side was the most persuasive and discuss why. Invite

the panel members to talk about the effect of the assigned role on what they said and how they felt about collective bargaining.

3. Identify a problem area in your assigned clinical setting that seems to be resistant to change. Write a new scenario for using a power-based change strategy to resolve the problem. Evaluate the effectiveness of the power-based strategy, the risks involved in using it, and how willing you would be personally to become involved in and/or lead the change initiative. Refer back to the other frameworks for change and compare them with the power-based approach.

4. Interview a union delegate, union organizer, and/or the representative of either the state or local nurses' association regarding the pros and cons of collective bargaining. Compare their answers with the responses of first-line managers, supervisors, and nursing administrators. Whose argument do you find most convincing? Apply the questions from critical analysis to their argument in reaching your conclusion.

CHAPTER 22
POLITICAL AND ECONOMIC
CONTEXT OF HEALTH CARE

I. CONTENT OUTLINE

II. LEARNING OBJECTIVES

After completing this chapter, the reader will be able to:
- Trace the evolution of the U.S. health care system from the mid-nineteenth century to the present.
- Assess the impact of various payment mechanisms on health care and health care delivery.
- Discuss the current issues and concerns related to the present health care system.
- Create scenarios for continued evolution of the health care system through the twenty-first century.

III. NOTE TO INSTRUCTOR

Some students, particularly those who have had little experience or interest in politics, will find this chapter's perspective new. It is critical to impress on them that the political and economic trends discussed in this chapter directly affect their practice and their nursing career. Inviting colleagues who have been active in politics and/or in the professional organizations is often helpful in this regard.

Many new terms and many complicated issues are addressed in this chapter. If students can personalize these (e.g., by seeing the effect on themselves and on people they care about), they will find it easier to appreciate how important these issues are.

IV. STUDENT LEARNING ACTIVITIES

A. Questions for Review and Discussion

1. What sources of help were available to people in colonial America?
2. How and by whom were hospitals used in the late 1800s?
3. How and by whom did the idea of health insurance develop?
4. What programs were established by the Social Security Act of 1935?
5. What is the difference between Medicare and Medicaid?
6. What effect did technological advances and research in the mid-twentieth century have on health care delivery?
7. Why did the Clinton health care reform movement fail?
8. What is a DRG? What effect did the establishment of DRGs have on reimbursement of health care costs?
9. What effect has the Baby Boomer generation had on health care so far? What future impact is expected?
10. What is the difference between retrospective and prospective payment for health care services?
11. What is an HMO? Capitation? Gatekeeper? How have they affected health care delivery recently?
12. Explain how PPOs and POSs are seen as alternatives to HMOs.
13. Explain how the recent changes in the health care system may lead to gridlock in the system.
14. What age group has the largest proportion of uninsured members? Why is this age group most likely to be uninsured? Why has this group increased in size recently?
15. Discuss the Jackson Hole Group's health care reform concept and the reasons that many opposed it. What issues remain unresolved?
16. What can nurses do to influence the health care system to (1) protect the health and welfare of their clients and (2) ensure the future of the nursing profession?

B. Projects/Assignments

1. Buy a copy of a local or national daily newspaper. Clip every article pertaining to health, health care, and health care delivery. List the titles of all the articles and summarize the content of each in one or two lines. What did this exercise tell you about current attitudes toward these subjects? What trends do you see for the future?

2. Attend a public hearing on a health-related issue. What arguments were made for and against the issue? Which side was the most persuasive? Why? How would the outcome affect health care consumers? How would it affect nurses as health care providers?

3. Write your own set of two contrasting scenarios for the way health care will be delivered in 2050 as shown in Chapter 22. Which one of the set do you prefer? Why? Which scenario do you think most people would prefer? Why?

4. It has been said that most health care professionals select for themselves the health care insurance option that allows the greatest choice of health care providers. Do you believe this is true?

5. Write a research paper on the emergence of HMOs and managed care. How did this movement begin? What was the original purpose? What effect have HMOs and managed care had on the health care system and on individuals seeking health care? What changes do you see occurring in the next 10 years in the delivery of health care?

6. Alternatively, write a case study on the interaction between a recently ill patient or friend and the health care delivery system. Evaluate the ways in which the system worked and the ways in which it failed the individual. Compare your case study with those of your classmates. What patterns emerge? What types of changes do you think are called for based on your analysis of these case studies?

CHAPTER 23
LEADERSHIP ASPECTS OF
CAREER DEVELOPMENT

I. CONTENT OUTLINE

OBTAINING A POSITION
The Job Search
Preparation
Basic Qualifications
Levels of Competence
Strengths and Weaknesses
Preferences
Opportunities
Resumes
Format
Essentials of a Résumé
Education
Work History
Skills and Experience
Summary of Highlights
Additional Tips
The Interview
Preparation
Traditional Interview
Interviewer Questions
Competency-Based Job Interviews
Applicant Questions
After the Interview
STAGES OF A NURSING CAREER

Stage 1: Getting Started
Orientation
The Honeymoon
Avoiding Reality Shock
Conflicts
Additional Pressures on the New Graduate
Ineffective Coping Efforts
Preventing Reality Shock
More Effective Coping
Stage 2: Getting Experience
Avoiding Burnout
Factors Contributing to Burnout
Counteracting Burnout

Stage 3: Advancement
Stage 4: Influence
Moving along the Career Path
SUMMARY

II. LEARNING OBJECTIVES

After completing this chapter, the reader will be able to:
- Conduct an effective job search.
- Design an appropriate résumé.
- Participate in both traditional and competency-based job interviews.
- Describe approaches to prevention and treatment of reality shock and burnout.
- Describe a career path for a nurse who has advanced to the highest level of the profession.

III. NOTE TO INSTRUCTOR

This is another new chapter written for the fourth edition. The focus is on the intrapersonal and interpersonal aspects of career development. It is not concerned with forecasts of shortages or projections about the specialties that will be most in demand in the future. Since these numbers and projections change rapidly, the best way to address them is by using the most recent government and professional organization data, most of which are now accessible online. Students can learn how to do this themselves—and develop a valuable skill for the future at the same time.

Given the wide age range and varied backgrounds of today's students, each class will respond differently to this chapter. Some will have a great deal of job-hunting experience and need little help developing a resume or handling a job interview; others may not. Some may have given a great deal of thought to their future careers; others may be confronting these decisions for the first time. Some may be caught up in the latest trend; others will be determined to chart their own course. Some individual guidance may be as valuable as group discussion.

IV. STUDENT LEARNING ACTIVITIES

A. Questions for Review and Discussion

1. What is a career path? How does this concept help you pursue career planning?
2. What are the three questions you should ask yourself when you begin your job search?
3. What types of qualifications are sought by employers of new graduate nurses?
4. List Benner's five levels of clinical competency in nursing and explain each one. At what level are you now?
5. What is the most effective way to go about finding job openings?
6. What categories of information are essential in a résumé? What should you put in the summary or highlights section?
7. What are the most common mistakes people make in preparing their résumés? How can you design your résumé to market yourself most effectively to a prospective employer?

8. What should you know about your prospective employer before the job interview?

9. Compare and contrast the traditional job interview with the competency-based interview. Which do you think is more challenging?

10. What do most prospective employers want to achieve during a job interview? What is she or he especially looking for during the interview?

11. What should the interviewee try to achieve during a job interview? What should you look for? What should you ask? What red flags should you be particularly alert for?

12. What are the most common "turnoffs" in job interviews? How can you avoid these?

13. Describe the four stages of a nursing career. What stage are you in now?

14. Why is an orientation important to a new employee? What should be included in an orientation for a new graduate? For an experienced nurse?

15. What is reality shock? When does it usually occur? How do professional ideals and work realities differ? How can reality shock be prevented?

16. How can a new graduate successfully make the transition from student to employee?

17. What is burnout? What factors contribute to its occurrence? How can you avoid becoming burned out? How can you counteract if you experience burnout?

18. Describe Stage 3 and Stage 4 of a nursing career. How does a nurse achieve these levels? Why would you want or not want to reach Stage 4?

B. Projects/Assignments

1. Invite an expert in competency-based interviews to class to demonstrate how these interviews are conducted in real life. Alternatively, role-play competency-based job interviews during a class session. Flip a coin to decide who will be the interviewer and who will be the job candidate. Use the cases in the chapter as a basis for making up others to challenge the "candidate." Ask the class to critique both the interviewer's and the interviewee's effectiveness and to provide suggestions for improving their technique.

2. Prepare a "winning" résumé as suggested in this chapter. Divide the class into groups of four to six students each to share résumés and offer suggestions for improving them. Alternatively, submit the résumés to the instructor for feedback.

3. Create your own list of personal and professional strengths and weaknesses as if you were preparing for a job search. How would you respond to this list if you were a prospective employer? How can you enhance your strengths and improve in areas of weakness?

4. Refer to the list of questions in the Preferences section of Chapter 23. Answer each question in writing. Then summarize what you have learned about yourself and your career goals.

5. Draw a career path for yourself beginning with the present year and extending all the way to the age of retirement. Be sure to include any twists and turns of the path that you expect to experience along the way, as well as any forks in the road and any barriers that you expect to encounter.

6. Do an online search for information about current job prospects in nursing. Consult with your librarian if you have difficulty finding the information you need after trying the Web addresses in the book and whatever search engines are available to you.